W9-BBG-846

Bubbles Rainbows & Worms

Science Experiments For Pre-School Children

Bubbles Rainbows & Worms

Science Experiments For Pre-School Children

By Sam Ed Brown

Illustrations by Silas Stamper

Gryphon House, Inc.
Mt. Rainier, Maryland

© **1981 by Sam Ed Brown**

ISBN 0-87659-100-4
Library of Congress Catalog Card No. 80-84598

Published by Gryphon House, Inc., 3706 Otis Street, Mt. Rainier, Maryland 20822. All rights reserved. No part of this publication may be reproduced, stored in a retrieval system, or transmitted, in any form or by any means, electronic, mechanical, photocopying, recording or otherwise, without the prior written permission of the publisher. Printed in the United States of America.

Design by Cynthia Fowler

Brown, Sam Ed., 1932—
    Bubbles, rainbows & worms.

    Includes bibliographies.
    1. Science—Study and teaching (Preschool)—Handbooks, manuals, etc. 2. Science—Problems, exercises, etc.
—Handbooks, manuals, etc. I. Title. II. Title: Bubbles, rainbows, and worms.
LB1140.5.S35B76   372.3'5'044   80-84598
ISBN 0-87659-100-4 (pbk.)   AACR2

Contents

The Young Child and Science

"Why did that happen? Why does it work that way? What can I do to change that? and What will happen if...?" Young children daily ask these questions about the world around them. Adults help young children teach themselves about science. Preschool science concerns the process rather than the product. With adults and older children, teaching may be verbal. This is not so with young children. To truly understand the definition of a word, children must have physically acted upon a concept in which the word was used. A concept has true meaning for children when they have actually tested it by exploration and manipulation.

Children do not have to be taught to explore, question, and manipulate; they are born with a powerful desire to do so. This need to handle, manipulate, and explore has been called many things by different psychologists and educators, who suggest that this drive sets the stage for all future learning. Children generate satisfaction from being able to manipulate and control materials and results outside their own bodies. This drive leads to a clarification and understanding of their physical world.

As children investigate the properties of the physical world, they add new knowledge to their accumulated store. As more knowledge is acquired, it becomes the foundation for new developing concepts. By handling, manipulating, tasting, feeling, and much more, the children are able to accommodate much of this information into pre-existing concepts. Thus, children broaden and deepen their understanding about the world about them. Children broaden their concepts about weight and mass as they float objects in a container of water. They better understand air pressure and movement as they drop feathers and watch them float to the ground. An insight concerning life processes is gained as children are allowed to care for animals and plants.

The need to teach science in preschool is not directed by a need to train future scientists and engineers for the future (although we may be doing this). Rather, it is an attempt in this modern, complex world to equip the child with basic survival skills.

In this age of dwindling resources, emphasis must be put upon conservation rather than disposal. If we are to teach conservation, then we must help children to understand the properties of the world around them. It is only through the understanding of the physical properties of air, water, soil, weather, and other natural phenomenon around them that these future citizens can hope to solve the ever-mounting problems facing the world.

A Word about Preschool Science for Teachers

At the present time both teachers in kindergarten and daycare, and parents of the children being taught, feel pressure to return to the basics, i.e. reading, writing, and arithmetic. As a result, the teaching of science in preschool is often approached on a haphazard basis through the use of filmstrips, field trips, demonstrations and ditto sheets, and not taught at all by parents. The teaching of preschool science should be a time of fun and discovery for both adult and child.

Materials for teaching

It is easy to acquire teaching materials for preschool science. They are all around. Common ordinary materials are ample for teaching science. Take for example, the container of milk served at lunch. Where does the milk come from? This question alone may lead into a complete unit on cows, farm animals, animal babies, products produced by animals, or domestication of animals. All this from one question! This does not even consider the question of how the milk gets to the school, what happens to it before, how it is made safe to drink, what is added to it, or who buys it. Not to mention why it has to be made safe, why we drink it, other animals that give milk, humans being mammals, what mammals are and why mammals give milk. And still we haven't even looked at nutrition, the container itself, the print on the container, storage of the milk and many, many other concepts.

Young children do not learn from something that does not interest them, they simply brush it aside. Young children are mostly interested in materials and objects that attract them and capture their attention. Little boys and girls frequently have things in their pockets that are of no value to anyone else: a colored rock, a marble, some glass, a bent nail, a piece of plant and, perhaps (wonder of wonders) a snake skin or mashed, dried frog. Teachers should be quick to capitalize on the natural curiosity of young children by providing a discovery or "science" table. This is a table where a child may bring treasures to show off to the class (properly labeled with the child's name). It is a joy to see a child hard at work trying to find the picture of a plant brought in by looking through seed catalogs and books containing pictures of common plants of the region.

The point here is that there is really no "special" equipment or supplies needed for an effective program in science. Let the children supply the majority of the materials needed for the program. At times it will be necessary to ask the children to bring in special things for an experiment. However, these items are seldom expensive and most parents are eager to supply such things as salt, flour, bluing, ammonia, nails, tacks, etc.

Use real objects, familiar to the child, for teaching

As can be gathered from the above discussion we are talking about the use of real, concrete objects when we talk about teaching preschool science. It is necessary for a child to have the object so that he can actively feel and see the properties of the object.

The problem with using elaborate, "do not touch," materials for a classroom demonstration is that children will get little from the demonstration because they do not know the materials. Again, this is why we use common, everyday objects. If a teacher is going to introduce new materials to the preschool child, the new materials must be left out for the children to explore before they are used.

Materials must relate to the real world

The author once watched a preschool teacher do an elaborate experiment with a beautifully designed model of the solar-system complete with sun, planets, and moons that revolved around the planets. The object was to explain to the children where "shooting stars" came from and why we could see them. While the children may have enjoyed watching the globes spin around, the lesson did nothing to increase their knowledge of the solar system. Not only had the teacher worked with objects that they knew nothing about (even though she did identify them verbally), but the teacher talked about things that were not really a part of the child's world. The real world in this case is that world with which the child has sustained day to day contact. Preschool teachers, to be successful, must be able to project themselves into the world of the child and be able to see things as the child sees them. Children can identify the sun, heat, light, health, growth, and night and day. After the child knows what the sun is and does, then one may begin with the rotation of the planets. Teachers sometimes forget that everything is new and wonderful to the young child.

The child must be presented with an orderly sequence of facts

Programs that are the most successful with young children, such as developed by Maria Montessori, are ones that seek to develop a curriculum that is both orderly and sequential. While adults are more successful in dealing with unrelated facts, they still have difficulties. Programmed learning kits have proved to be highly successful with adults. Both, and especially the young child, learn best with an orderly, sequenced curriculum.

Fitting Science into a Preschool Classroom

The teaching of science in preschool does not always have to be treated as a separate subject. Science can be a part of many other kinds of learning with preschoolers. Consider, for example, language development. If the language development lesson for the day is directed toward verbal descriptions of shapes and likenesses and differences, this would offer an excellent opportunity for a lesson on fruits and seeds. Fruits such as apples, oranges, bananas, peaches, and others could be examined, tasted, felt, smelled, and described by the children. Facts such as which fruits have seeds that may be eaten (bananas) and which ones do not, and which fruits have skins that may be eaten (peaches, apples) and which ones do not may be discussed. Other subjects such as differences in color, texture, shape, place where grown, and many more may also be questioned, talked about, discussed and described.

Another example might fall into the area of fine-motor development. Instead of having children work on commercial puzzles, the teacher might take a carrot and construct a puzzle by dividing the carrot into several pieces. Allowing the children to work with puzzles such as this will help children to understand how parts make a whole (parsnips or turnips might also be used).

Teaching children

How do we teach children? The answer is that we do not really teach the children, we provide an environment that encourages and allows the children to teach themselves. This environment must be rich and sustaining to promote growth and learning.

Modeling is a powerful teaching tool. Learning takes place as the young child observes the attitudes, habits and actions of the teacher. An example would be the care of plants in the classroom. The young child observes the attitude toward plants that the teacher displays. Children observe how the teacher cares for plants, not necessarily how they are told to care for them. The teacher often creates an atmosphere for learning through modeling.

Teachers must also provide the needed emotional support and love that will allow children to come to value themselves as worthy and successful. Children must be rewarded for success and for appropriate behavior so that they might learn that there is justification for their behavior and positive value for learning.

TEN COMMANDMENTS FOR TEACHING SCIENCE TO CHILDREN

1. Give every child a chance to be a part of the experiment with special emphasis on the use of the senses.
2. Make everything as non-threatening as possible.
3. Be patient with children.
4. Allow the children to control the time you spend on an experiment.
5. Always use open-ended questions.
6. Give children ample time to answer questions.
7. Don't expect "standard" reactions and "standard" answers from children.
8. Always accept divergent answers.
9. Be sure to encourage observation.
10. Always look for ways to extend the activity.

The Classroom Science Center

A science center is an integral part of any preschool classroom. The amount of equipment a teacher is able to afford for the center is not as important as the amount of interest and enthusiasm generated within the children. It is very important that the children know that the teacher is interested in things that they are interested in and wonder about, and feel encouraged to bring things to the classroom to be shared with the class. After the children are sure that it is all right to bring things in, the classroom will soon have a collection of beautiful and wonderful items. These items of interest to children may range from rock collections to mashed bottle caps.

Setting up the center

As most teachers do have access to some equipment and supplies, the following large items are suggested:

At least two long tables
A bookcase
An aquarium and fish
An ant farm (may be child-made)
Shelves for storage and display
Large metal or plastic tub
Rugs on the floor
Large stool magnifier

Small equipment

As discussed earlier, most things needed for preschool science can be furnished by the children. However, a few of the necessary items that could be on hand are:

Different size coils of rope
Measuring devices
Magnifying glasses
Scales: balance and spring
Small and large mirrors

Location of the center

The location of the science center often depends on the space available. There are certain factors that should be taken into consideration, however, such as the general ebb and flow of the children in the room. The science center should be located, if possible, out of the general traffic flow. For example, it should not be located in an area where it is necessary for children to pass through or by on their way to lunch. Some activities such as growing crystals could be tempting to some children not involved in the experiment. It must be, however, in a clearly defined space. One good method is to block the area off using book or toy shelves.

The science center is a "touch and do center," not a place for display. It is possible to find beautifully arranged, well-equipped centers in some kindergartens that are for visitors only. The author has examined some centers that showed the outline of the objects in dust when they were moved.

First, and most importantly, the center must attract children. It must be a place where children want to work. If children are not eager to be in the science center it is probably because it is not interesting to them, not that they are not interested in science.

Children are eager to learn. Children especially love the science center if it offers interesting things to see, do, smell, taste, and feel. Any teacher can have a successful center and be successful teaching science if she lets herself think like a child and will permit herself to wonder and not be afraid to learn with the children.

The activities in this book are specifically designed for preschool children. The selection of these activities is designed to stimulate teachers to begin with basic experiments and go from there. Each activity presented may be extended indefinitely.

GOOD LUCK!

Use of Vocabulary

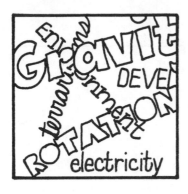

Included with each of the experiments in this book is a section called WHAT TO TALK ABOUT. This section gives the teacher suggestions for questions and topics to discuss.

Because young children are very verbal, they bring a wealth of words with them to any particular activity. Many of the words in the young child's vocabulary may be words of which they are unsure. Through experimentation and usage, children learn definitions and refine the use of these previously undefined words. It is also very important that children learn the particular vocabulary associated with a particular concept.

For these reasons, a teacher should not limit her vocabulary when speaking of a concept because she fears that the words used are too hard for the child. Some words that are difficult for children must be used because they are the only words that will apply. For example, when teaching the child about gravity, one cannot expect the child to understand what causes gravity. The child can, however, learn how gravity affects objects that are dropped. Gravity can become a part of the vocabulary of the young child even though the child cannot explain the concept.

Teachers must strive for language enrichment, and a key element of language enrichment is a wide use of different words.

Materials that Teachers Might Collect and Add to The Science Center

balls
heavy and light string
different textured cloth
paper of various kinds and sizes
sink plungers
glasses (glass and plastic)
cans with tops off
rock salt
corks
plastic tubing
rubber tubing
liquid detergent
powdered detergent
straws
crayons
paper cups
construction paper
tempera paint
adhesive spray
talcum powder
balloons
books about animals
books about plants
egg cartons
pins

sticks
sponges
charcoal
potting soil
rocks
springs
salt
food coloring
prism
milk cartons
assorted wheels
assorted nails
assorted magnets
lamp
scissors
glue
thumbtacks
pencils
markers
paper sacks
plastic sacks
rubber gloves
screen wire
fishing weights
hot plate

Experiments With:

Air

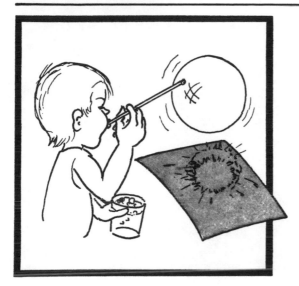

Blowing Bubbles

What You Are Going to Teach: Air is a real substance and has weight. Light sometimes changes color when it passes through water. Science can be fun.

Materials Needed for Teaching: Liquid detergent, straws, cups, construction paper, crayons.

What You Do: Put a small amount of soap and water into cups so that each child has a cup of soapy water. Dip the end of the straw into the cup, remove straw allowing the soapy mixture to drip once. Blow gently and produce a bubble. Talk about air being inside of the bubble. Talk about how the bubble has different colors because light changes when it shines through the bubble. Ask the children why they think bubbles burst when they hit the ground.

When it is time to finish this activity, allow the children to catch some of the bubbles on a piece of construction paper. Talk about why the popped bubble leaves a wet circle. Allow the children to draw around the wet outline and color designs.

What to Talk About: Bubbles, pop, liquid, blow, colors, circle.

An Explanation of Principles: Light is broken into different wave lengths as it passes through water, allowing the different colors to be seen. Wet rings on the construction paper show that a bubble is composed of water surrounding air.

Which Is Faster?

What You Are Going to Teach: Air is all around us. Air affects the way things move.

Materials Needed for Teaching: Two pieces of typing paper and a chair to stand on.

What You Do: Wad up one piece of paper in a ball. Talk to the children about how the wadded paper and smooth piece are alike/different. Ask the children if they think they weigh the same. (A simple balance scale may be used). Ask the children whether, if you dropped both of them, they would fall together? Climb on a chair, hold one piece of paper in each hand and drop them. Why does the wadded-up piece fall faster? Explain to the children that as the flat piece of paper falls, it has to push through the air and more of the surface is exposed to the air. Since there is more air pushing and putting pressure on the flat piece of paper, it falls more slowly.

What to Talk About: Surface, air, pressure, wadded, flat.

An Explanation of Principles: Children sometimes think that the larger (or heavier) an object is, the faster it will fall. The reasons some things fall faster than others is due to the amount of friction (drag) from the air.

Air, Air, Everywhere

What You Are Going to Teach: Air is real. Air has substance.

Materials Needed for Teaching: Pan of water, balloons, plastic bag, straws, empty plastic bottle.

What You Do:
1. Put an empty plastic bottle into a pan of water and watch the bubbles.
2. Blow up a balloon and put it under the water, release the air in the balloon.
3. Allow the children to feel the air coming from a straw when they blow through the straw.
4. Allow the children to blow through the straw into the water.
5. Blow up a balloon. Place the mouth of the balloon into the mouth of a plastic bag. Let the air escape from the balloon into the plastic sack.

What to Talk About: Bubbles, transfer of air.

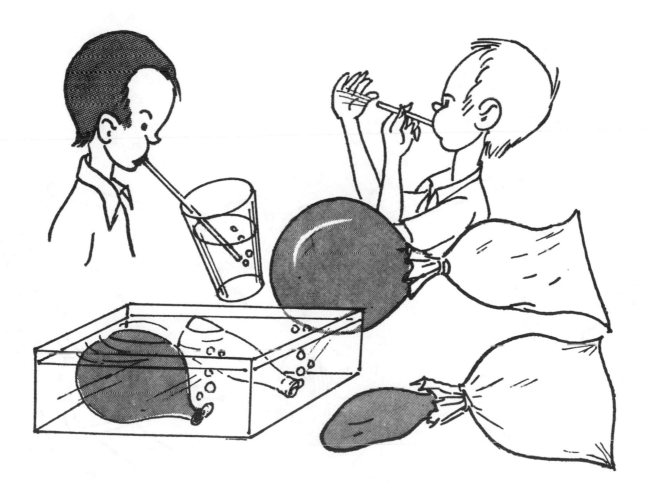

Plumber-Plumber

What You Are Going to Teach: Air is real. Air has body and weight.

Materials Needed for Teaching: Two plumber's friends (drain plungers).

What You Do: Allow the children to explore a plumber's friend. Talk about what it is used for. Take two plumber's friends and push them against each other until they stick. Let the children handle the plumber's friends. Why are they stuck together? What happened to the air when they were pushed together?

What to Talk About: Suction, air pressure, vacuum.

An Explanation of Principles: When a drain plunger head is forced flat against a surface by pushing down on the handle, the air is forced out of the rubber head creating a vacuum. The pressure of the air on the outside of the plunger head is so strong that the head will stay stuck until some air seeps in. In the case of two plunger heads pushed against each other, a larger and stronger vacuum is created and the air pressure from both sides will hold them together.

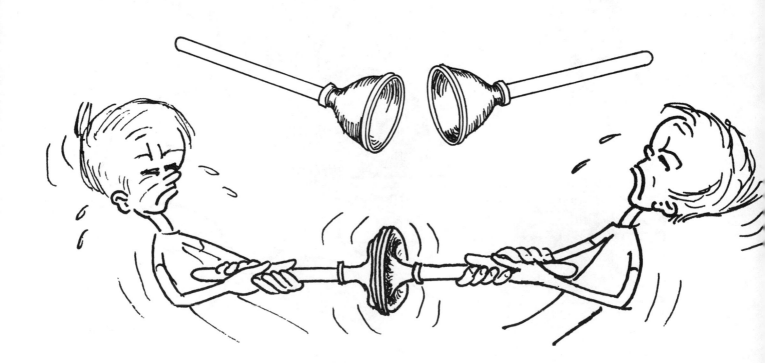

Blow the Man Down

What You Are Going to Teach: Air is real and can move objects.

Materials Needed for Teaching: Tin can, straws, balloons, rubber bands, paperback book.

What You Do: Stand an empty tin can on a table and let the children try and blow it over. Now tell the children you are going to blow it over. Attach a balloon to the end of a straw with a rubber band. Sit the can on top of the balloon. Blow through the straw and the balloon will fill, tipping the can. Stand a book on end and let the children try to blow it over. Now place the book on a sack. Blow into the sack tipping over the book. Allow the children to do this.

What to Talk About: Talk about how the air fills the balloon and sack and pushes over the tin can and book.

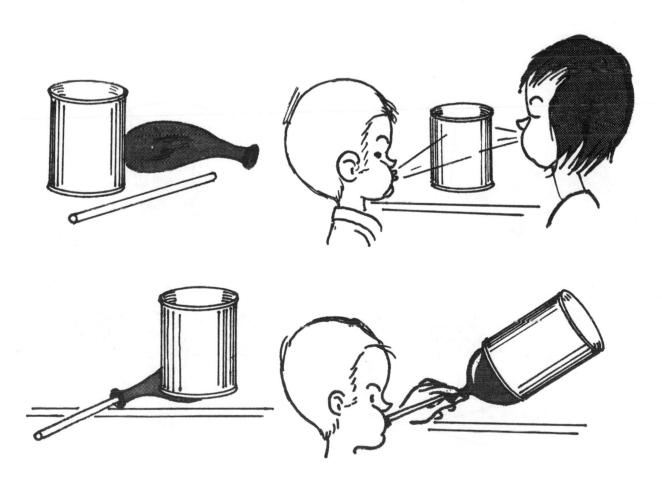

Wet and Dry

What You Are Going to Teach: Air takes up space. Air has substance.

Materials Needed for Teaching: A clear plastic drinking glass, a pan of water, paper towels.

What You Do: Tell the children that you are going to try to put a paper towel under the water without getting the towel wet. Crumple up a paper towel and put it in the bottom of the glass. Push the glass completely underneath the water, open end first. Be sure the glass is not tilted. When the glass is lifted out of the water, the paper will be dry. Again, push the glass with the paper in it beneath the water. This time allow the glass to tilt and let the children see the air escape and water replace the air. This time the paper will be wet.

What to Talk About: Air pressure, replacing air with water, compression.

An Explanation of Principles: When a glass is forced straight down into the water, the air inside the glass cannot escape and is compressed in the glass. The compressed air will not allow the water to reach the paper. When the glass is tilted, the air escapes and is replaced by the water.

Children's Books About Air

Keats, Ezra Jack. **Whistle for Willie.** New York: Viking Press, 1964.

Mizumura, Lazue. **I See the Winds.** New York: Crowell, 1966.

Scarry, Richard. **Great Big Air Book.** New York: Random House, 1971.

Selsam, Millicent. **Plenty of Fish.** New York: Harper & Brothers, 1960.

Tresselt, Alvin. **Follow the Wind.** New York: Lothrop, Lee, & Shepard, 1950.

Zolotow, Charlotte. **When the Wind Stops.** New York: Harper and Row, 1962.

Experiments With:

Animals

Animal Baby Puzzles

What You Are Going to Teach: Matching. Animal babies look much like their parents.

Materials Needed for Teaching: Scissors, glue, strips of posterboard or heavy paper, magazines, old story books.

What You Do: Spend some time with the children finding pictures of animals and babies. Cut these pictures out. Select pictures of animals and pictures of the same animals with babies. Glue the picture of the adult animal on one end of a strip of posterboard and the picture of the baby animal on the other end of the strip. Cut the strips in half in different ways to produce puzzles. Mix several strips together and let the children match the correct animal with the correct baby.

What to Talk About: Animals, babies, matching, growing, adults.

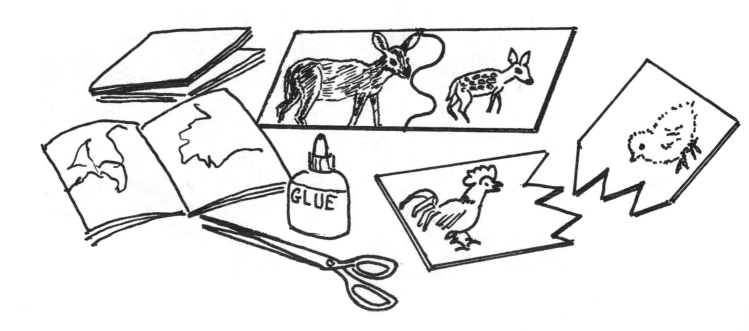

Hunting for Animals and Insects

What You Are Going to Teach: Insects and animals require care.

Materials Needed for Teaching: An aquarium with a screen on top, a small cage or other suitable container for animals and/or insects.

What You Do: From time-to-time children bring insects into the classroom from outside. Children also like to bring a pet to school occasionally. Teachers may provide a place for children to care for pets or study insects.

What to Talk About: Where does the animal/insect live? What does the animal/insect eat? What do they do? What special care is needed?

An Explanation of Principles: Different units can be developed depending on whether the children have brought in insects or animals. Children need to learn, while they are very young, to value animal and plant life. Insects should be kept for only a short period of time before being released. Teachers should model correct behavior toward insects and animals.

Watching Ants

What You Are Going to Teach: Ants live in families, ants care for eggs.

Materials Needed for Teaching: One gallon clear glass jar, ant hill, digging tool, dark paper, cotton.

What You Do: Fill a clear glass jar about one-half full of dirt. Take your children on a science walk to find an ant hill. Observe the ants coming and going to the hill carrying food. After talking about the ant hill and how a family of ants lives together in the hill, dig up the ant hill, including the surrounding dirt and debris, and place it all in the jar. Place dark paper over the top of the jar to encourage the ants to go underground. A piece of wet cotton on the dirt that is kept damp will supply the ants with all the moisture they need. The ants may be fed once or twice weekly by adding crumbs of cookies or bread to the jar. Occasionally, you should add a spoon of honey to the jar.

What to Talk About: How ants live in families, what ants eat. How ants store and care for their eggs. How each ant seems to have a specific job.

An Explanation of Principles: When a clean glass jar is used, children will be able to observe tunnels that are close to the sides. Like other insects, ants should only be kept for a short period of time in an artificial environment. Ants should not be kept longer than a month.

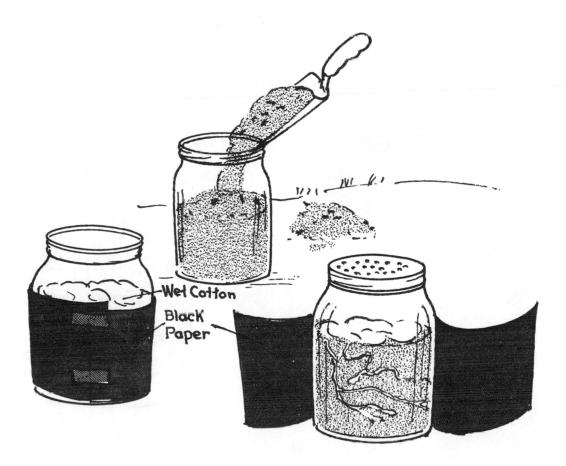

Wet Cotton

Black Paper

Wild Spiders

What You Are Going to Teach: Spiders (and other small animals) can live and reproduce in captivity.

Materials Needed for Teaching: Plaster of Paris, wire cylinder (rolled up wire or screen-tied), two disposable cake pans, sticks, sponge, spider.

What You Do: Build a cage for the spider. Put a small amount of plaster of Paris into a cake pan. Place the wire cylinder on its end into the plaster of Paris. After it is dry, place a wet sponge, some sticks, and a spider in the cylinder. Cover the top with a pie pan. Occasionally it will be necessary to add some insects for the spider to eat.

What to Talk About: Spider, captivity, sponge, plaster of Paris, insect homes, reproduction.

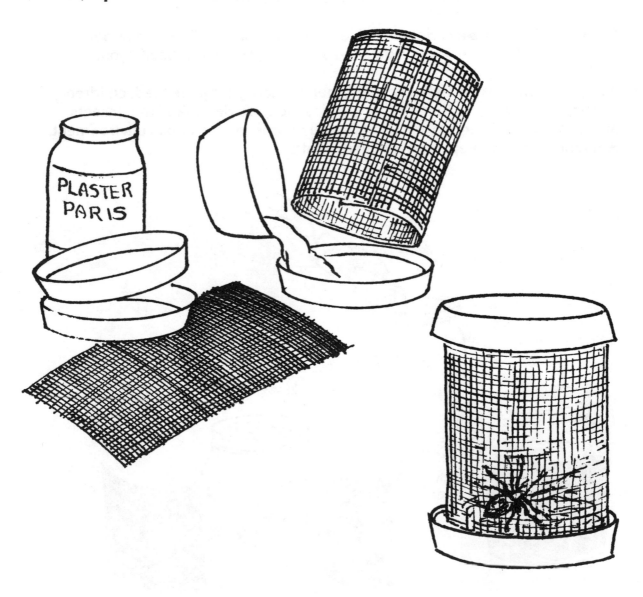

Spider Webs

What You Are Going to Teach: Spiders make their webs from substances in their own bodies. Different spiders make different webs. Spiders use sticky webs to catch food.

Materials Needed for Teaching: Black construction paper, talcum powder, spray adhesive.

What You Do: Take the children on a walk to hunt spider webs. Locate a spider web in the building or outside on the bushes. Help the children sprinkle talcum powder on the web and carefully lift the web up with the paper until it is free and on the paper. Spray with spray adhesive. Look for webs that are different.

What to Talk About: How spiders spin webs to catch insects. How spiders eat these insects. How the web is sticky so the insects will stick to the web.

An Explanation of Principles: Spiders secrete the sticky material from their bodies to build webs. Different spiders build different types of webs. The library will have books with pictures of spiders and webs.

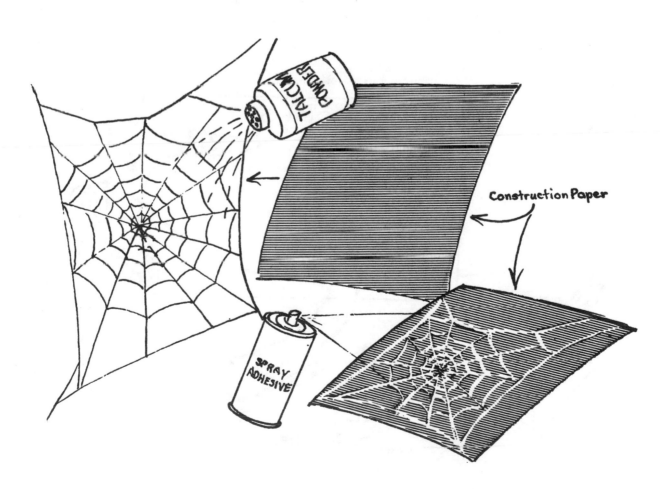

Construction Paper

Animal Homes

What You Are Going to Teach: Animals have homes. Different kinds of animals have different kinds of homes.

Materials Needed for Teaching: Pictures of animals, pictures of animal homes, yarn, glue, posterboard.

What You Do: From magazines, allow the children to cut pictures of animals and homes where animals live. Divide the posterboard in half. On one half glue the pictures of the animals. On the other half glue pictures of animal homes. Cut yarn into two-foot lengths. With a hole punch, punch a hole beside each picture. Attach one end of the string to a picture of an animal. Encourage the children to find the home that belongs to that animal and attach the other end of the string to the correct hole, i.e., bird and nest.

What to Talk About: The different names of animal homes such as nest, burrow and hill. Talk about where animals are found, as in jungle, cave, water, etc.

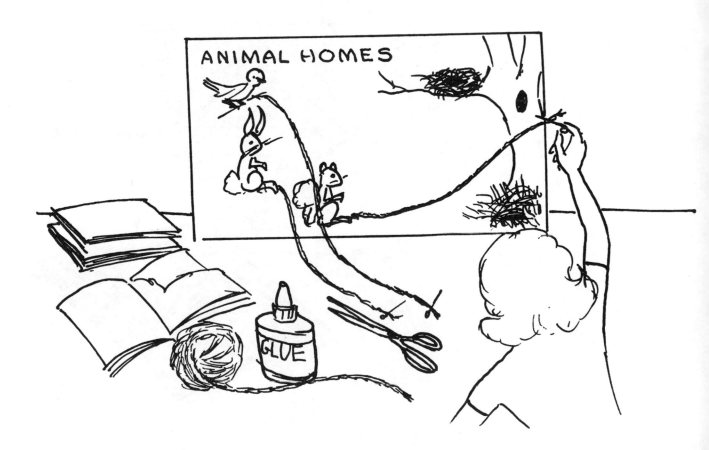

Earthworms

What You Are Going to Teach: Different living things need different environments for living.

Materials Needed for Teaching: Large (one-two gallon, three-six liter) glass jar with a large mouth, soil, earthworms, gravel, food for worms (lettuce, cornmeal, cereals).

What You Do: Mix a small amount of gravel in good rich soil. Put earthworms into the jar. Add food on top of the dirt and keep the soil moist. Children can observe the earthworms in an environment much like the one in which they live.

What to Talk About: The way the worms burrow and live underground. How they adapt to their new environment.

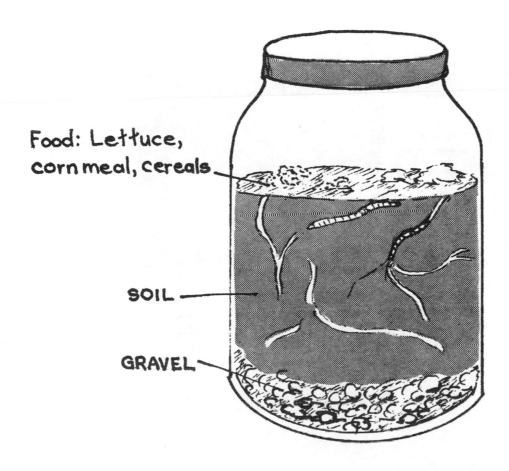

Food: Lettuce, corn meal, cereals

SOIL

GRAVEL

From a Tadpole to a Frog

What You Are Going to Teach: Not all baby animals look like their parents. Care of animals.

Materials Needed for Teaching: A water tank or water container (a one-gallon, three-liter jug will do), some frog eggs, pond water and plants, green leafy vegetables.

What You Do: Put the frog eggs, pond water, and plants in your container. Watch daily for eggs to hatch. After the eggs begin to hatch, supply green vegatables for food for the tadpoles. Let the children observe that tadpoles do not look like frogs. Let the children continue to watch as the hind legs and front legs begin to grow and the tail grows smaller.

What to Talk About: The changes taking place, hatching the eggs. What frogs and tadpoles eat. How frogs and tadpoles breathe.

An Explanation of Principles: Rocks should be supplied so that the tadpoles can climb up for air as they grow. If you use a gallon jug for egg hatching, it would be better to change containers as the tadpoles develop.

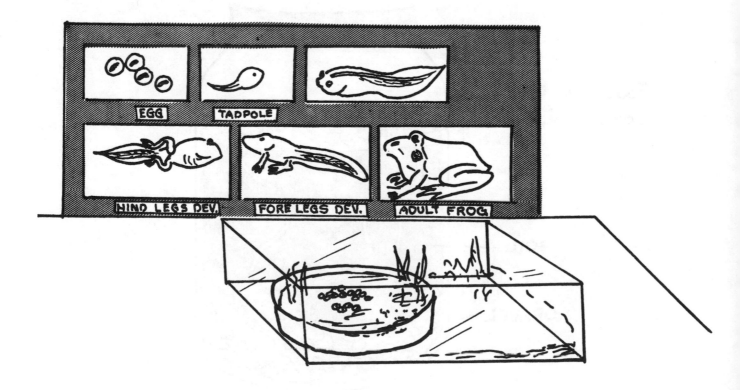

Terrariums

What You Are Going to Teach: The creation of an environment for growing plants. Demonstrate to the children that plants can use the same air and water over and over again.

Materials You Need for Teaching: A large one or two gallon (three to six liter) glass jar or a quart size (one liter) glass jar for each child, sand, soil, gravel, and a small lid to hold water.

What You Do: A large terrarium or individual terrariums may be made. Instruct the children to cover the bottom half of their jars with gravel. Next have the children mix soil and sand together, one part sand and four parts soil, and place a layer of the soil mixture on the gravel. Small plants such as ferns and moss may be planted in this soil. Put some water in a small lid and set it in the jar so the plants may have water. Various decorations may be added such as colored gravel or miniature animals. Screw the lid on tightly and the terrarium is complete.

What to Talk About: Talk about how the plants reuse the same air and water. Talk about the way animals breathe in oxygen and breathe out carbon dioxide. Tell the children that plants breathe carbon dioxide and give off oxygen.

An Explanation of Principles: A simple explanation is enough for young children. They will understand more about plants as they see that neither air or water has to be added to the plant's environment.

Children's Books
About Animals

Bancroft, H. and Van Gelder, R. **Animals in Winter.** New York: Crowell, 1963.

Carle, Eric. **1, 2, 3 to the Zoo.** New York: Collins, 1968.

Carle, Eric. **The Rooster Who Set Out to See the World.** New York: Franklin Watts, Inc., 1972.

Carle, Eric. **The Very Hungry Caterpillar.** New York: Collins, 1970.

Conklin, Gladys. **I Caught a Lizard.** New York: Holiday House, 1967.

Conklin, Gladys. **I Like Butterflies.** New York: Holiday House, 1960.

Conklin, Gladys. **I Like Caterpillars.** New York: Holiday House, 1958.

Conklin, Gladys. **We Like Bugs.** New York: Holiday House, 1962.

Darby, G. **What Is A Frog?** New York: Benefic Press, 1967.

Grabianski. **Grabianski's Wild Animals.** New York: Franklin Watts, Inc., 1969.

Graham, M. **Be Nice to Spiders.** New York: Harper & Row, 1967.

Lionni, Leo. **Fish Is Fish.** New York: Pantheon Books, 1970.

Lionni, Leo. **Inch by Inch.** New York: Obolensky, 1960.

Lionni, Leo. **Swimmy.** New York: Pantheon Books, 1963.

McCloskey, Robert. **Make Way For Ducklings.** New York: Viking Press, 1969.

Selsam, Millicient. **All Kinds of Babies.** New York: Four Winds, 1967.

Selsam, Millicient. **Animals As Parents.** New York: Morrow, 1965.

Selsam, Millicient. **Terry and the Caterpillars.** New York: Harper & Row, 1962.

Tresselt, Alvin. **The Beaver Pond.** New York: Lothrop, Lee and Shepard, Co., 1970.

Tresselt, Alvin. **"Hi, Mister Robin!"** New York: Lothrop, Lee and Shepard, Co., 1950.

Ungerer. **Tomi.** Crictor. New York: Scholastic Book Services, 1970.

Wildsmith, Brian. **Birds.** New York: Franklin Watts, Inc., 1967.

Wildsmith, Brian. **Fishes.** New York: Franklin Watts, Inc., 1968.

Windsmith, Brian. **Python's Party.** New York: Franklin Watts, Inc., 1975.

Windsmith, Brian. **Wild Animals.** New York: Franklin Watts, Inc., 1967.

Experiments With:
The Environment

Wind Vanes

What You Are Going to Teach: The wind blows from different directions. We can record which way it blows.

Materials Needed for Teaching: Straight pin, drinking straw, arrowhead (cut an arrowhead with a long shank from cardboard), feather, pencil with eraser, long stick.

What You Do: In one end of a straw, put a feather and in the other end, put a paper arrowhead (fold the shank of the arrowhead and push into straw hole). Put the pin through the straw with the point going on into the eraser of the pencil. Tie the pencil to a long stick. Children may take their wind vanes outside. Help the children keep a record on a daily basis of which way the wind is blowing. Is there a relationship between the way the wind is blowing and the weather? The temperature?

What to Talk About: The different directions the wind blows from (north, east, south, west). Relationships between the difference of the wind and the weather and temperature.

An Explanation of Principle: It is sometimes difficult for young children to understand how a wind vane works. You may demonstrate by blowing on the feather that the air (wind) will force the wind vane to turn until the wind no longer hits it from the side. When the wind vane has turned to where the wind no longer hits the feather, the arrow is pointing toward you.

Silhouettes

What You Are Going to Teach: Properties of light and shadow. Self-awareness. Small muscle control.

Materials Needed for Teaching: Dark construction paper, thumbtacks, glue, scissors.

What You Do: Thumbtack a sheet of paper to the wall. Place a lamp on the table in front of the paper. Place a chair sideways between the lamp and the paper and have the child sit in the chair looking forward. Trace the outlines of the child's silhouette on the paper. Allow the child to cut out and mount the silhouette on dark-colored construction paper. What made the shadow?

What to Talk About: Talk about how the shadow is made. Have children ask other children if their silhouette looks like them.

Making a Compass

What You Are Going to Teach: How to construct a simple magnet. How a compass works. Why we use compasses.

Materials Needed for Teaching: Cork, needle, pan of water, magnet.

What You Do: Stroke a pin 30 to 50 times with a magnet, always in the same direction. This will magnetize the pin. This can be demonstrated by picking up other pins with the magnetized pin. Insert the pin through a cork and float the cork in the water. Which way does the pin float? If you lift it out of the water and put it back, will it point the same way?

What to Talk About: Talk about the North Pole. Talk about the mineral deposits that attract magnets found in the north. Discuss how knowing this can help a person that is lost.

An Explanation of Principle: Magnets are attracted to the north due to the large mineral deposits found there.

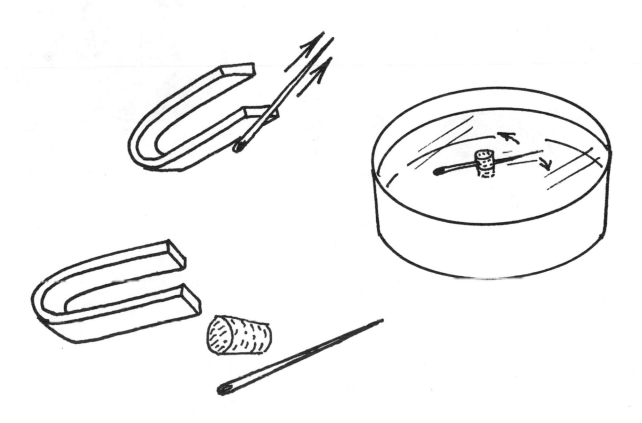

Making Lightning

What You Are Going to Teach: Electricity can be made. This static electricity can be seen.

Materials You Need for Teaching: Two balloons, wool cloth, a dark room.

What You Do: Blow up the balloons. Rub one balloon briskly on a piece of wool. Push the balloon against the wall. Explain to the children that static electricity created by rubbing the balloon on wool is causing the balloon to stick to the wall. Tell the children they can also see this static electricity. Darken the room and rub both balloons briskly on the wool. Hold the balloons, almost touching, and the children can observe a spark jump between the balloons.

What to Talk About: Ask the children if they have ever been shocked after walking on a carpet or putting on a sweater.

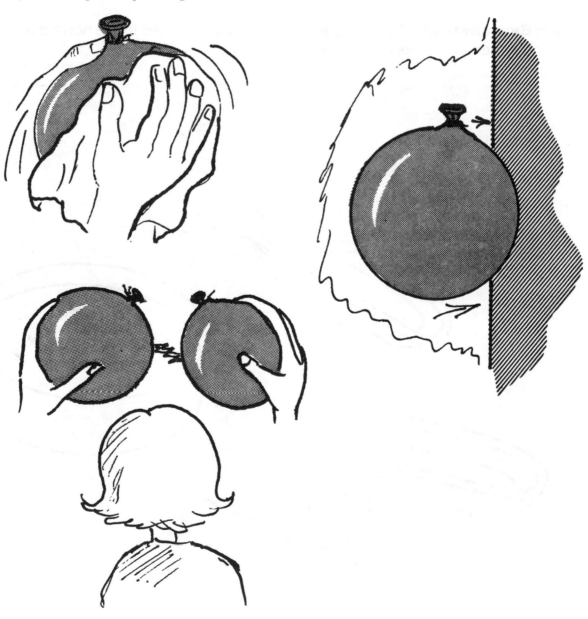

Static Electricity

What You Are Going to Teach: That static electricity may be created by friction.

Materials Needed for Teaching: A piece of wool. A balloon. A comb. Small pieces of paper.

What You Do: Have the children blow up the balloon. Ask the children to put it against the wall and see if it will stick. Now rub the balloon on the wool. See if it will stick. Explain what is happening when you rub the balloon on wool. Using a pocket comb, ask a child to comb her hair when it is very dry. Then ask the children if they can use the comb as if it were a magnet to pick up small pieces of paper. What happens? Why?

What to Talk About: Static electricity, produce, magnet, wool.

On Charting Temperature

What You Are Going to Teach: Temperature can be measured with a thermometer. Temperature changes from day-to-day and changes during the day.

Materials Needed for Teaching: A large thermometer. A piece of posterboard.

What You Do: Introduce the thermometer to the children. Practice with them until they can read the temperature. Using posterboard, make a chart so that the temperature may be recorded daily at certain specified times. Let the children take turns recording the temperatures each morning and each afternoon.

What to Talk About: Different scales are used to record temperature—centigrate (or Celsius) and fahrenheit. Mark the thermometer at 32ºF (0ºC) and talk about water freezing. Mark the thermometer at 212ºF (10ºC) and talk about water boiling.

DATE		8:00AM	2:00PM	DATE		8:00AM	2:00PM
FEB	1	30	40	FEB	16		
	2	33	45		17		
	3	28	39		18		
	4	26	32		19		
	5	31	45		20		
	6	35	44		21		
	7	43	55		22		
	8	39	45		23		
	9	35	43		24		
	10	28	35		25		
	11	34	40		26		
	12	39	55		27		
	13	40	59		28		
	14						
	15						

Parachute Game

What You Are Going to Teach: This experiment helps to show that air, even though you don't normally see it, is an object itself. Air affects the way objects behave.

Materials Needed for Teaching: A small ball, a string and a two-foot square of cloth.

What You Do: Allow the children to throw the ball into the air and catch it. Now explain to the children that if they had some way to catch some of the air it would make a difference in the way the ball fell. Tie a string around the ball, tie the string to the four corners of the cloth. Fold the cloth and throw the cloth and ball into the air. The parachute should float down.

What to Talk About: The cloth will fill with air. Since air is an object, it will cause the parachute to fall slowly.

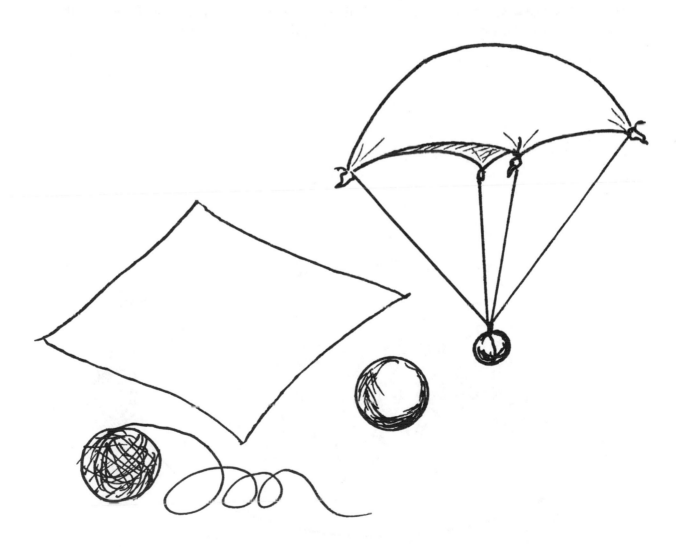

Night and Day

What You Are Going to Teach: Differences between night and day. Different activities are appropriate for these times.

Materials Needed for Teaching: No special materials.

What You Do:

1. Form your children into a circle facing out, symbolic of children around the world. Assign one student to be the sun. Let that student carry a yellow circle cut from construction paper. The sun should walk very slowly around the circle. As the sun moves around the circle, those children who cannot see the sun (night) must pretend to sleep. Those children that can see the sun may engage in activities normally engaged in during daylight hours without leaving the circle.

2. Have all the children close their eyes and let one tell about something that happens at night. Have your children open their eyes and let one child tell about something that happens during the day.

What to Talk About: Talk about differences in night and day. Talk about what different things the children do during the night and day.

Learning About the Sun

What You Are Going to Teach: The sun gives us light and heat. Sunlight can burn.

Materials You Need for Teaching: Thermometer, magnifying glass, black construction paper.

What You Do:

1. Discuss the difference the sun makes in our skin color over the course of the summer. Why? Talk about being sunburned. Let one child explain to the other children what it is like to be sunburned. Go outside on a warm, sunny day. Stand in the sun and feel the heat. Why does the skin become warm? Stand in the shade. Is there a difference? Why?

2. Use two pieces of black construction paper. Leave one inside, keep one outside in the sun when it is not raining. Is there a difference in the color? Why?

3. Show the children how you can burn paper using a magnifying glass.

STRONGLY CAUTION THE CHILDREN THAT IT CAN ALSO BURN THEIR SKIN. DO NOT LET THE CHILDREN USE THE MAGNIFYING GLASS OUTDOORS WITHOUT CONSTANT ADULT SUPERVISION.

What to Talk About: Talk about the heat given off by the sun. Talk about the shade and the difference in temperature.

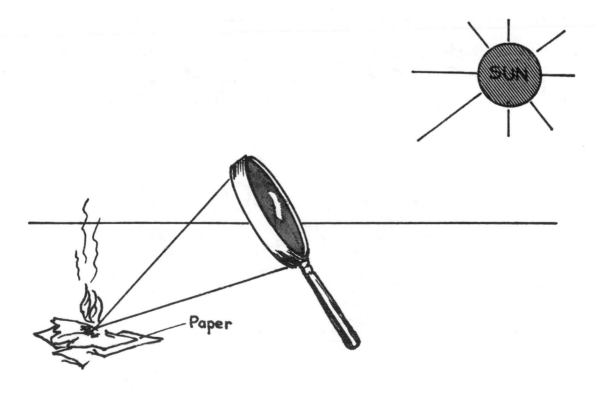

Paper

Rotation of the Earth

What You Are Going to Teach: The sun shines from different directions during the day. Rotation of the earth.

Materials Needed for Teaching: A globe, a ball to represent the sun, small wooden blocks for markers, a stick.

What You Do: Talk to the children about how the sun seems to rise in the east and set in the west. Demonstrate what is happening by rotating the globe next to the ball. On the playground, set up a stick in the morning so that it casts a shadow. Let the children mark the end of the shadow with a small block. Allow the children to use other blocks to mark the end of the shadow each hour.

What to Talk About: Why did the shadows change? When was the shadow longest? When was the shadow shortest?

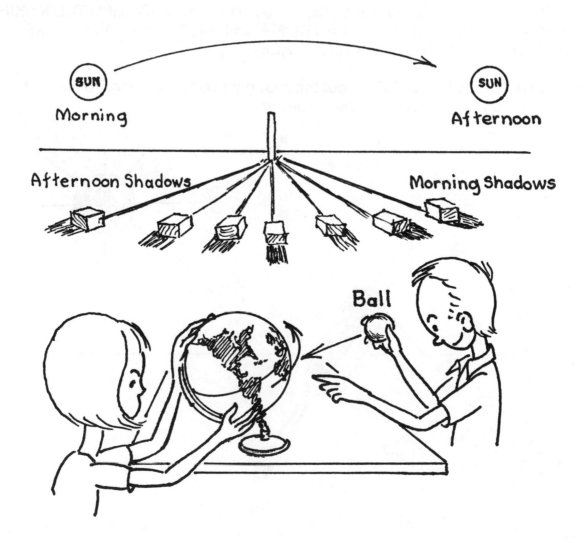

Dressing for the Seasons

What You Are Going to Teach: Different weight and textured materials are worn for different seasons.

Materials Needed for Teaching: An assortment of dress-up clothes including heavy and light coats, raincoats, sweaters, shorts, short sleeve shirts, gloves, overshoes, etc. A full length mirror, a hand mirror.

What You Do: Arrange the clothes in the house-keeping center. Use racks or clothes trees. Try to put footwear together, hats together, etc. Divide the children into four groups. Ask each group to dress as they would dress in one of the four seasons: Spring, Fall, Winter, Summer. Let each group explain why they dressed the way they did. Have the children observe the different textures and weights of the clothes.

What to Talk About: Talk about the weather—hot, cold, cool, warm. Talk about the seasons and what kind of temperatures are associated with each season. Talk about the textures and weights of clothes.

Seasons

What You Are Going to Teach: The association of different clothing with different seasons.

Materials Needed for Teaching: Old catalogs, magazines, scissors, glue, posterboard.

What You Do: Help the children make a seasons poster. Talk about what the weather is like. What is the season? Using a piece of posterboard divided into four squares, label each square for a different season and paste a picture appropriate to the season next to the label. Let the children use catalogs and magazines to find pictures of different types of clothing. Allow the children to cut the pictures from magazines and paste them in the appropriate block.

What to Talk About: What clothes are appropriate for each season? How do these clothes differ? Why do we wear heavy clothes in winter? Ask questions and discuss each season and clothing worn.

Gravity

What You Are Going to Teach: Properties of gravity.

Materials Needed for Teaching: An assortment of small items such as a block, a pencil, scissors, toys.

What You Do: The young child can easily learn that whatever is dropped will fall. However, it is a bit much to expect the very young child to be able to explain why. We can lay the foundation of future understanding. We may use the falling of a block structure as a learning experience. Which way did the blocks fall? If you drop a pencil, will it fall up or down? Will it ever fall to the side? Drop several objects to the floor such as a block, pencil, scissors or toy. Which ones fall up and which ones fall down? Have the children hold a small wooden block out at one's arm getting tired holding the block.).

What to Talk About: Use the word gravity as you talk about things falling. Explain that gravity is a force that can't be seen but can be felt (Explain about their arm getting tired holding the block.).

Children's Books
About the Environment

Aliki. **My Visit with the Dinosaurs.** New York: Crowell, 1972.

Baylor, Byrd. **Everybody Needs a Rock.** New York: Scribner's Sons, 1974.

Bradfield, Roger. **Hello, Rock.** Wisconsin: Western Publishers, 1965.

Branley, F. **What Makes Day and Night?** New York: Crowell, 1961.

Bulla, Clyde R. **What Makes a Shadow?** New York: Scholastic Book Services, 1962.

Burningham, John. **Seasons.** New York: Bobbs-Merrill, 1970.

Duvoisin, Rodger. **The House of Four Seasons.** New York: Lothrop, Lee, & Shepard, 1956.

Feravolo, Rocco. Junior **Science Book of Magnets.** New York: Scholastic Book Services, 1967.

Hoban, Russell. **Bedtime for Francis.** New York: Harper & Row, 1960.

Keen, Martin. **How and Why Wonder Book of Magnets and Magnetism.** New York: Grossett and Dunlap, 1963.

Knight, David C. **Lets Find Out About Magnets.** New York: Franklin Watts, Inc., 1967.

Lobel, Arnold. **Frog and Toad Together.** New York: Harper & Row, 1972.

McGovern, Ann. **Stone Soup.** New York: Scholastic Book Services, 1971.

Experiments With:

Plants

Seed Party

What You Are Going to Teach: Plants produce seeds which, in turn, produce plants. Different plants have different seeds.

Materials You Need for Teaching: An assortment of fruits such as an orange, apple, lemon, cantaloupe, small watermelon, peach, cherry, etc. A package of sandwich bags. A magic marker. Pictures of fruits cut from magazines.

What You Do: Let the children take turns carefully cutting the fruits and taking out some seeds. Talk about how the seeds are alike and different. Put the different seeds into plastic sandwich bags and label accordingly. Later, match the seeds to the pictures. If you extend this activity over several days, the children may enjoy the fruit at snack time or may make a fruit salad. This activity may also be done with vegetables. There are many seed catalogs with beautiful pictures.

What to Talk About: Talk about differences in seeds and plants. Discuss plant growth and what is necessary to grow healthy plants. Talk about seeds that are eaten and those that are not eaten. Children may want to plant some of their seeds.

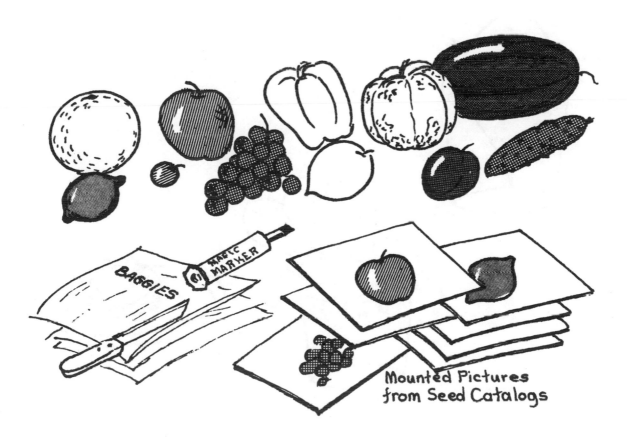

Mounted Pictures from Seed Catalogs

Growing Without Seeds

What You Are Going to Teach: All plants do not grow from seeds.

Materials Needed for Teaching: A variety of plants that will root themselves in water, such as sweet potatoes, carrots, or vines.

What You Do: Take a jar about three-fourths full of water and place a sweet potato in the water so that only the bottom one-third of the potato is in the water. Toothpicks put into the side of the potato and laid across the mouth of the jar will keep the potato from slipping further into the water. Next, cut the top off of a carrot that has already had the greens removed. Place the carrot top in a shallow dish of water, flat side down. Observe that both plants produce roots and leaves.

What to Talk About: Some plants grow from seeds, and some from cuttings.

Planting Beans

What You Are Going to Teach: The relationship of sunlight and water to growing plants.

Materials Needed for Teaching: Three flower pots, a soil mixture: ½ potting soil, ¼ garden soil, ¼ sand. Nine dried beans.

What You Do: Talk with the children about how plants grow and the kinds of help they need to grow. Be sure to discuss both sunshine and water. Explain to the children that together you all will determine if sunshine and water are really necessary for growing plants. Fill three flower pots with a good soil mixture. Children should help you mix soil. Plant three beans in each pot. Put two pots on the window ledge so that they both can get sun. Keep the soil in one pot moistened so that it does not dry out. Do not add water to the second pot. Put the third pot in the closet where it will not get sunshine and keep the soil moist. Observe the growth of the plants.

What to Talk About: Talk about what happens when plants do not receive water. Talk about what happens when plants do not receive sunlight.

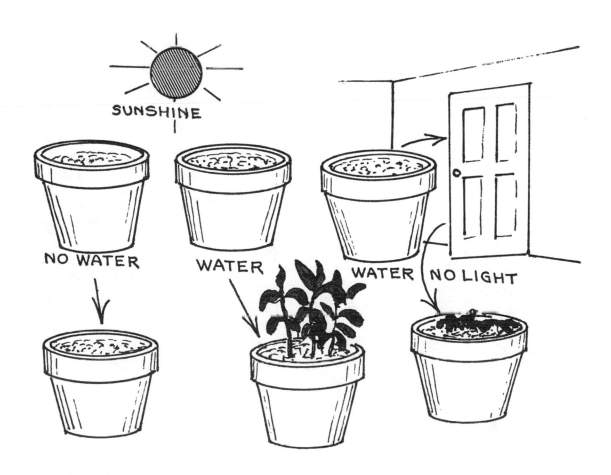

SUNSHINE

NO WATER   WATER   WATER   NO LIGHT

Growing Beans

What You Are Going to Teach: How a seed germinates, sprouts, and grows.

Materials Needed for Teaching: Small glass jars (baby food jars are excellent), lima beans or other type beans, cotton, water.

What You Do: Arrange so that each child has a baby food or other type jar. Put a strip of tape with the child's name on each jar. (Older children may write their own names.) Put cotton in the bottom of each jar (about ¼ full). Put two beans between the cotton and the glass in each jar and two beans on top of the cotton. Dampen the cotton and keep damp. Place the jars on the window ledge so they will receive light. Watch what happens!

What to Talk About: Talk about the sprouting of the beans, and the growing of the roots and other parts of the plant as it grows.

Development

What You Are Going to Teach: There is a sequence of growth in plants and animals. Sequencing.

Materials Needed for Teaching: A series of pictures showing the development of a plant from a seed, and a series of pictures showing the development of an animal from an egg (chicken, frog).

What You Do: Do one (plants or animals) at a time. It is probably better to begin with plants. Make a bulletin board of the pictures in the correct sequence. Talk daily about the development. Let the children tell the story of the development. Code the pictures with numbers on the back. Put the pictures in random order on the chalk ledge. Allow different children to put the pictures in sequence.

What to Talk About: Talk about plants developing from seeds. Make comparisons and contrasts between animals and plants as they develop.

Making a Seed Book

What You Are Going to Teach: Matching seeds to parent plants. Classification and grouping.

Materials Needed for Teaching: Construction paper, manila paper, stapler, magic marker, glue, scissors, old seed catalogs and magazines.

What You Do: Allow each child to construct a seed book. To construct the book use a piece of construction paper as the cover. Lay two pieces of manila paper on top of the construction paper, fold all in half and staple on the folded edge. The child should collect seeds and glue them to a page along with a picture of the plant that she has cut from a seed catalog or magazine. Label each page with the name of the plant and help the child with any other notes or observations she might wish to add.

What to Talk About: Talk about seeds, plants, matching, books, and vocabulary related to growing plants.

Children's Garden

What You Are Going to Teach: Developing a positive attitude toward living plants. We may grow our own food.

Materials Needed for Teaching: A plastic or metal dishpan, or a shallow wooden box. Be sure there is a hole in the bottom of the pan or box. A package of potting soil. Some sand. A variety of garden seeds (mustard greens, radishes, lettuce, peas, kale, etc.).

What You Do: Explain to interested children what they can do. Let the children help mix the soil: ½ potting soil, ¼ sand, and ¼ garden soil that the children dig for themselves from outside. Prepare the soil and talk with the children about what should be planted and why. Try to follow the children's suggestions on what to plant. Tending the garden will be a long-term project.

What to Talk About: Planting food, tending plants, mixing soil, vegetable names.

An Explantion of Principles: This activity is described as an indoor activity because many schools do not have space that may be used for a garden. For schools that have outside space, this would also be a good outside activity. Plants could be started indoors and then transferred outside. If there is room outdoors, children may plant popcorn in the fall. This may be harvested after the first frost. Children love to rub two ears together to get it off the cob and then have the teacher pop it, and eat it—a favorite snack.

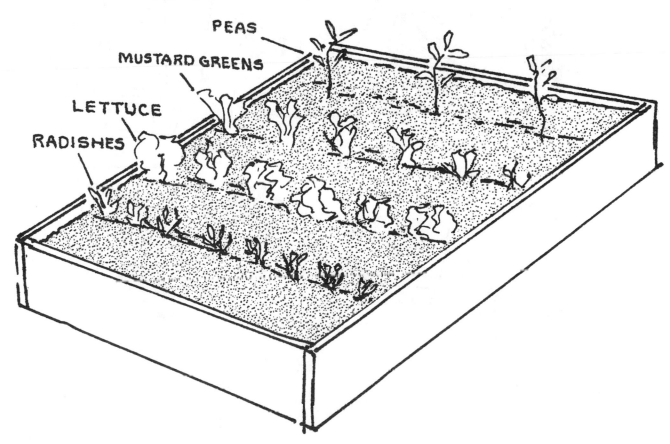

PEAS
MUSTARD GREENS
LETTUCE
RADISHES

Seeds and Fruits

What You Are Going to Teach: The association of seeds and the fruits and plants that grow from these seeds. The names of different fruits and plants.

Materials Needed for Teaching: Seed catalogs, scissors, glue, posterboard.

What You Do: Allow the children to cut pictures of fruits and plants from seed catalogs. Mount the pictures on a piece of posterboard. Ask the children to bring in seeds that match the pictures. Purchase from the seed store those seeds the children might have difficulty finding. Mount the seeds on small pieces of cardboard and keep them in the science center so that children might match the seeds with the pictures.

What to Talk About: Names of plants and fruits. Differences between seeds. Shapes.

An Explanation of Principles: It may be difficult for young children to match seeds with plants especially if they are much alike. A teacher should supply for this activity a variety of plants and seeds that are quite different (apple, lima bean, watermelon, peach, avocado).

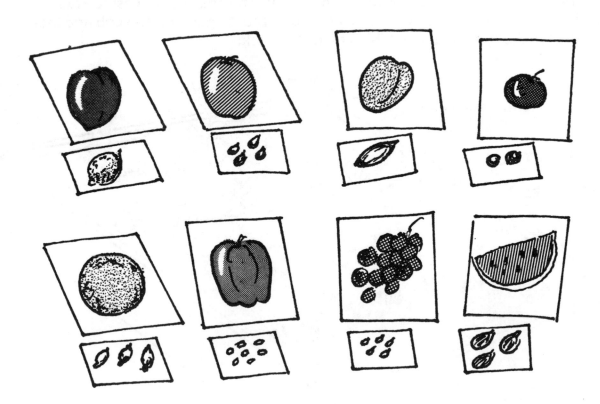

Children's Books About Plants

Benton, William and Elizabeth. **How Does My Garden Grow?** Wisconsin: Western Publishers, 1969.

Howell, Ruth. **A Crack in the Pavement.** New York: Antheneum, 1970.

Selsam, Millicient. **Maple Tree.** New York: Morrow, 1968.

Selsam, Millicient. **The Plant We Eat.** New York: Morrow, 1955.

Selsam, Millicient. **Seeds and More Seeds.** New York: Harper & Row, 1959.

Tresselt, Alvin. **The Dead Tree.** New York: Parents Magazine 1972.

Children's Books—Nature:

Barr, George. **Young Scientist Takes a Walk.** New York: Whittlesey House, 1959.

Hoban, Tana. **Look Again.** New York: Macmillan, 1971.

Selsam, Millicient. **How to be a Nature Detective.** New York: Harper & Row, 1966.

Simon, Mina L. **Is Anyone Here?** New York: Antheneum, 1967.

Experiments With:
The Senses

Washing and Feeling

What You Are Going to Teach: The properties of the sense of touch.

Materials Needed for Teaching: Warm water, doll clothes, liquid soap, a clothesline.

What You Do: Let the children gather up the doll clothes in the housekeeping center. Encourage the children to wash all the clothes. First, wash in plain water. How does it feel? Do the clothes feel differently? Now allow the children to use liquid soap on them. Rinse the clothes. How do they feel? Hang them on a line. How do they feel as they begin to dry?

What to Talk About: The different ways the clothes feel. Why we wash clothes. What soap is for. Why we hang the clothes on a clothesline.

Sounds Around Us

What You Are Going to Teach: Different things make different sounds.

Materials Needed for Teaching: Chalk, pen, paper, zipper, jar with screw lid, bell, book, etc.

What You Do: This activity is designed to make children aware of the fact that different things have sounds of their own. Listening is a learned skill. The first step in teaching this skill is to make children aware of sounds. With a group (taking turns) or with an individual, have a child close his eyes. While eyes are closed, wad up the paper. The child should try and identify the sound. Use other objects and repeat.

What to Talk About: Talk about how sounds are different (soft, sharp, loud).

Music Everywhere

What You Are Going to Teach: How sounds are produced. What affects the production of sound.

Materials Needed for Teaching: A square cake pan. Assorted width rubber bands.

What You Do: Place the rubber bands around the cake pan. Pluck the different rubber bands and watch them vibrate.

What to Talk About: Does the vibration have anything to do with the sound? How do they vibrate for a loud sound? How do they vibrate for a soft sound? Does the width of the rubber band have anything to do with the sound it makes? What?

Explanation of Principles: The length of the rubber band, the width of the rubber band, and the placement of the rubber band on the pan determine the sound produced by the band. The sound is caused by the vibrations of the rubber band. Thick rubber bands produce lower sounds because they vibrate slower, and thin rubber bands vibrate faster causing a higher sound.

Hello, Who's There?

What You Are Going to Teach: The properties of sound. How sound travels.

Materials Needed for Teaching: Two plastic styrofoam cups, a long string, two toothpicks.

What You Do: Punch a small hole in the center of the closed end of each plastic cup. Insert the string through the hole in the plastic cup from the outside to the inside. Tie the end of the string around the toothpick and then pull. The toothpick will lie across the bottom of the cup, preventing the string from falling out. Do the same with the other cup and the other end of the string. Pull the string tight between the two cups. Let one child place his cup over his ear and another child speak into his cup. What happens? How is the sound traveling?

What to Talk about: Talk about how the sound travels along the string.

An Explanation of Principle: Sound travels from one cup to the other as the sound causes the string to vibrate. The vibrations carry the sound along the string. If the string is touched while it is vibrating it will disrupt the sound.

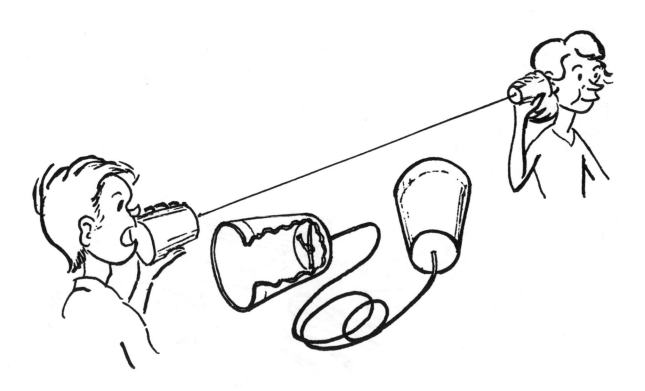

Tasting

What You Are Going to Teach: One of our senses is taste. We can distinguish between substances with this sense.

Materials Needed for Teaching: Foods that are salty, sweet, sour, bitter, spicy and bland. Carrots, pickle sticks, cheese cubes, radishes, raisins, grapefruit juice, chocolate milk, whole milk.

What You Do: Have a tasting party to acquaint the children with different tastes. Talk not only about how the food tastes, but also about the texture, appearance of the foods, and other features. Which ways do they look different? Do they smell different? Do they feel different? How are they alike?

What to Talk About? Salty, sweet, sour, bitter, spicy, bland, crispy, soft, hard, odor, shape.

What Is That Smell?

What You Are Going to Teach: Different things have different smells. We can use smells to identify substances. Smell is one of our senses.

Materials Needed for Teaching: Baby food jars, paper towels, vanilla extract, lemon extract, cloves, mustard, fried bacon, onions, etc.

What You Do: Put a wadded-up paper towel in the bottom of each baby food jar. Put a different subject for smelling in each jar. Allow the children, while blindfolded, to smell and guess what the odors are.

What to Talk About: Talk about the different smells. How are they alike and how are they different?

Exploring Odors

What You Are Going to Teach: Almost everything has an odor that can be detected through smell.

Materials Needed for Teaching: A variety of objects usually found in the classroom.

What You Do: Divide the children into pairs and let them take an "odor walk" around their room. Encourage them to smell objects they wouldn't expect to smell such as leather, blocks, paint, tables, rugs, pet cages, painted objects, sinks. Talk about what they have smelled. Classify objects into categories such as "smells good", "smells bad", "doesn't smell much", "smells like...."

What to Talk About: How different things smell different. Discuss why they smell different.

Touching

What You Are Going to Teach: One of our basic senses is the sense of touch. Different objects feel different and we can identify different objects by the way they feel.

Materials Needed for Teaching: Different textured objects such as silk, burlap, marshmallow, clay, metal, paper, sandpaper, etc.

What You Do: Lay all of the objects out so that the children may handle them and talk about them. Talk about the way they feel. Introduce vocabulary. Put the objects in a bag. Let a child put his hand into the bag and select an object by feel. Ask the child to describe the object. Is it hard? Soft? Rough? Smooth? Let the child guess what the object is.

What to Talk About: Talk about the feel of each object.

Children's Books About the Senses

Berkly, Ethel S. **Big and Little, Up and Down.** Mass.: Addison-Wesley, 1950.

Schlein, Miriam. **Shapes**. Mass.: Addison-Wesley, 1952.

Shapp, Martha and Charles. **Let's Find Out What's Big and What's Small.** New York: Franklin Watts, 1959.

Experiments With:

Water

Making Steam

What You Are Going to Teach: How water changes to steam.

Materials Needed for Teaching: A hotplate, a pan, a glass lid that will fit completely over the top of the pan, water.

What You Do: Explain to the children that they are going to try and do something different with water. **THIS EXPERIMENT MUST BE CLOSELY SUPERVISED.** Help the children fill the pan one-half full of water and bring it to a boil on the hotplate. Be sure the glass is on the pan. When the water begins to boil, droplets of water will form on the inside of the glass lid. The lid may be lifted so the children can see the steam. **CHILDREN MUST NOT ATTEMPT TO TOUCH THE STEAM AS SEVERE BURNS COULD RESULT.**

What to Talk About: Discuss with the children the fact that water turns into steam when it is boiled. Explain that the steam turns back to water as it cools and this causes the droplets of water to form on the lid.

M king Clouds

What You Are Going to Teach: Clouds are composed of water. Temperature affects cloud formation.

Materials Needed for Teaching: Glass container with a wide mouth (such as a restaurant size mayonnaise or pickle jar), hot water, ice cubes, lamp, flat glass cover for glass container.

What You Do: Pour about two inches of very hot water into the glass container, put the lid on and allow to sit for 3 to 9 minutes. Place ice cubes on the lid at the end of this time. Darken the room and hold a lamp behind the bottle. The children will observe the formation of a cloud in the bottle.

CAUTION: THIS EXPERIMENT SHOULD BE DONE ENTIRELY BY THE TEACHER WITH THE CHILDREN WATCHING FROM A SAFE DISTANCE AWAY. GLASS CAN BREAK AND HOT WATER CAN BURN!

What to Talk About: Why the clouds form. Talk about real clouds and how they form.

Explanation of Principle: As the moisture that has been vaporized cools because of the ice, it forms clouds of moisture. Real clouds form the same way. As moisture cools, it condenses and forms clouds.

(1) sit 3 to 9 min. (2)

ice cubes

(3)

Water and Ice

What You Are Going to Teach: Properties of water. Content of ice. Freezing.

Materials Needed for Teaching: Paper cups, water, rubbing alcohol.

What You Do: Winter, during freezing weather, is an excellent time to experiment with ice. Fill several cups with water and two cups with alcohol and mark the cups. Set the cups outside on the window ledge at the end of the day to remain out all night. Next morning, bring in the cups. What has happened? After the ice has melted, what is left?

What to Talk About: How cold weather freezes water to form ice. Different liquids freeze at different temperatures. Talk about adding antifreeze to a car in winter.

An Explanation of Principles: Most young children have already developed a relationship between cold weather and ice. Develop this relationship further by explaining that it has to be a lot colder to freeze some liquids. If we add a liquid that is hard to freeze to water, it makes the water harder to freeze. Talk about antifreeze.

Water Trick

What You Are Going to Teach: Air is real. Air can push and has weight.

Materials Needed for Teaching: A glass of water and a cardboard square large enough to fit over the opening in the glass.

What You Do: Fill a glass full of water. Turn the glass over and pour the water out in the sink. Tell the children that you can turn the glass over without the water coming out. Let the children guess how you will do it. Fill your glass about three-quarters full and place the cardboard square over the opening. Turn the glass over and the air will hold the cardboard in place and the water will remain in the glass. This will hold for only a short time. When the cardboard absorbs water it will fall out.

What to Talk About: Talk to the children about how air pushes on the cardboard.

Explanation of Principles: When the glass is turned upside down, a partial vacuum is formed in the glass. As air tries to fill the vacuum, the air pressure put on the paper holds it in place.

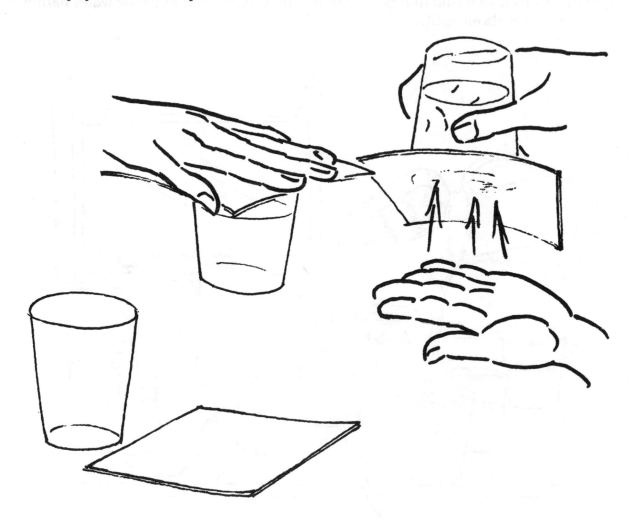

Floating Objects

What You Are Going to Teach: Some objects will float on water, some objects will not.

Materials Needed for Teaching: A shallow pan of water and assorted objects made of different materials. Two plastic trays, one with a picture of a floating object and one with a picture of an object sinking.

What You Do: Fill a shallow pan with water. Spread the objects you have collected on the table near the pan of water. Encourage the children to experiment to see which objects will float and which will not float. Will all the objects float? Encourage the children to sort the objects into trays according to whether they float or don't float.

What to Talk About: Ask questions about why the children think some things float and others don't. Talk about the materials and what they are made from. Compare the materials that float and sink for likenesses and differences.

Experimenting With Water

What You Are Going to Teach: Some properties of water. Water affects different substances different ways.

Materials Needed for Teaching: Kleenex, beans, sugar, salt, vegetable oil, different textures of cloth, different size tubes and funnels, water, and glass jars.

What You Do: Allow the children to explore what effect water has on different substances. Fill some small glass jars with water. Put a kleenex in one, some beans in another, some sugar in another, some salt in another, some vegetable oil in another, a nail in another and a marble or rock in another. Let the children observe what happens over a period of time. Pour water through different size funnels and tubes and observe the speed at which the water flows. Pour water on several different textures of cloth.

What to Talk About: Which things dissolve in water and which do not? Rust forms on the nail. Water flows through tubes and funnels. Water has a different effect on different textures of cloth.

Evaporation

What You Are Going to Teach: Some properties of air and water. The water will evaporate and be absorbed into the air if left exposed for periods of time.

Materials Needed for Teaching: Glass jar or shallow pan, water, marker.

What You Do: Place the glass jar or shallow pan in the science center. Fill the container of water about three-fourths full. Mark the level of the water. Each day mark the level of the water. In a few days the water will be gone leaving a small amount of sediment.

What to Talk About: Talk about how water is absorbed into the air through evaporation. Talk about moisture and humidity. Call the children's attention to the left-over sediment.

Explanation of Principle: The salts and other impurities will be left after the water evaporates.

Making Frost

What You Are Going to Teach: Changes in temperature cause dew. Frost is really frozen dew.

Materials Needed for Teaching: Tin can with lid removed. Rock salt, crushed ice.

What You Do: Allow the children to put two cups of crushed ice and one-half cup of rock salt in a can. Have the children stir the mixture rapidly. Go on to another activity and tell the children they will return in about thirty minutes. When you return, the outside of the can will have dew on it. If you wait a while longer, this dew will change to frost.

What to Talk About: Talk about where the dew came from and how it was formed. Also, talk about the dew changing to frost.

An Explanation of Principle: As the can cools, the moisture in the air condenses on the cool surface. As the can becomes colder, the water on the surface of the can freezes causing the formation of frost.

Fish Breathe

What You Are Going to Teach: Fish live in the water and breathe water the way we breathe air.

Materials Needed for Teaching: Fish tank and the accessories that go with the tank including food, etc. Water and fish.

What You Do: The only thing that the teacher must do is to be sure that the fish are properly cared for. Different children may be assigned the responsibility of feeding the fish and cleaning the tank whenever necessary. Proper care of fish is important and should be fully understood by children.

What to Talk About: Talk about the way fish breathe. Discuss their gills and how they are used.

Explanation of Principle: Fish use their gills to take in (breathe) the water. Oxygen is extracted from the water by the fish just as animals extract oxygen from the air with their lungs.

Children's Books About Water

Branley, F. **Snow Is Falling**. New York: Crowell, 1961.

Fisher, A. **I Like Weather**. New York: Crowell, 1963.

Holl, Adelaide. **The Rain Puddle**. New York: Lothrop, Lee, and Shepard, 1965.

Keats, Ezra Jack. **The Snowy Day**. New York: Viking Press, 1962.

Rosenfeld, Sam. **A Drop of Water**. New York: Harvey House, 1970.

Simon, Seymour. **Wet and Dry**. New York: McGraw-Hill, 1960.

Tresselt, Alvin. **Hide and Seek Fog**. New York: Lothrop, Lee, and Shepard, 1965.

Tresselt, Alvin. **Rain Drop Splash**. New York: Lothrop, Lee, & Shepard, 1946.

Tresselt, Alvin. **White Snow, Bright Snow**. New York: Lothrop, Lee, & Shepard, 1947.

Zolotow, Charlotte. **Summer Is**. New York: Aberland-Schuman, 1967.

Miscellaneous Experiments

Learning About Transportation

What You Are Going to Teach: Everyday concepts about ordinary transportation, traffic.

Materials Needed for Teaching: Small sticks, rags, tricycles, wagons, ropes, whistle, cardboard policeman's badge, tagboard.

What You Do: On an ungrassed section of your playground, scratch to outline roads, or on a grassy section mark roadways with small sticks with bits of cloth tied onto the sticks. Make traffic signals from tagboard: stop, yield, road construction, no right turn, etc. Appoint one child as traffic officer. After discussing the traffic signs and what they mean with the children, let the children "travel the roads" on their tricycles and wagons. The traffic officer should be sure that the signs are obeyed. This same physical setup may be used for a variety of games.

What to Talk About: Talk about the meanings of the traffic signs. Discuss why we have traffic laws. Discuss the role of police officers.

Transportation

What You Are Going to Teach: We use many different forms of transportation. Some people operate motor vehicles as an occupation.

Materials Needed for Teaching: Magazines that deal with transportation and ordinary magazines. Scissors, glue, construction paper.

What You Do: Allow the children to find pictures of different types of transportation: auto, taxi, plane, bus, vans, etc. Try to get two pictures of each. Also, have the children cut out pictures of people that operate these forms of transportation: bus drivers, pilots, taxi drivers, milkman, etc. Try to find two pictures of each of these. Pictures should be mounted on construction paper.
- A. Children may match transportation pictures.
- B. Children may match workers.
- C. Children may match driver to vehicle.

What to Talk About: Various transportation names, worker's names.

Roll On Big Wheels

What You Are Going to Teach: Simple machines. How machines help people. How people use machines.

Materials Needed for Teaching: Milk carton, four spools, two long nails, string.

What You Do: Tie a string to a milk carton. Allow the children to pull the milk carton along the top of a table. How hard is it to pull? Insert the nails through the spools and attach the milk carton. Now allow the children to pull milk carton. Is it easier? Why did people begin to use the wheel? If we add things to the milk carton does it make it easier or harder to pull?

What to Talk About: Wheel, machine, invent.

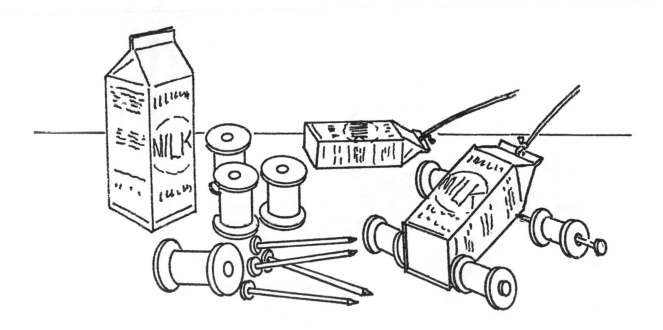

Creating Colors

What You Are Going to Teach: Through this activity the children will better learn the names of primary colors and learn that combinations of primary colors will create new colors.

Materials Needed for Teaching: Newspaper, white foam egg cartons with the lids removed, water, red, yellow, and blue food coloring.

What You Do: Cover a table with newspaper. Put out the egg cartons and fill the sections half full of water. Have the children put the primary food colors in three egg sections and encourage them to mix the colors. When mixed, they will create new colors.

What to Talk About: Discuss the primary colors (red, blue and yellow) and talk about how they may be used to create new colors.

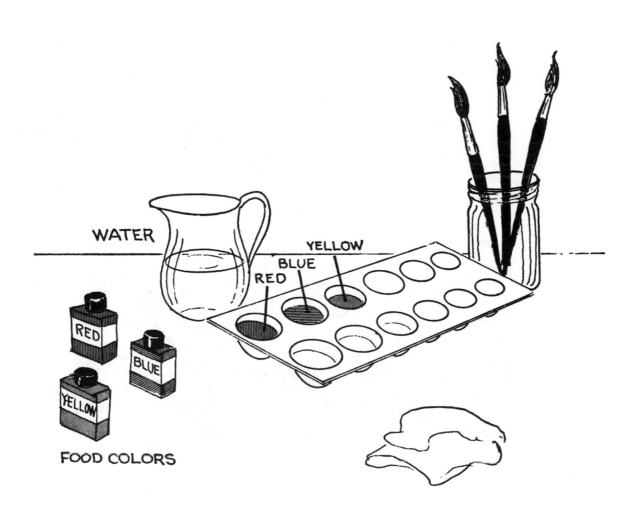

WATER

YELLOW

BLUE

RED

RED

BLUE

YELLOW

FOOD COLORS

Collections

What You Do: Allow the children to classify their collections by color and by shape. Provide picture books, dictionaries, cut out pictures, seed catalogs, shell books and other resources for the children to identify their collections.

What to Talk About: This depends on the collection.

What You Are Going to Teach: Most objects can be classified into colors or shapes, i.e., different colored leaves, different shaped shells, etc.

Materials Needed for Teaching: Depending on the time of the year and the section of the country in which you live, a variety of things may be collected. Leaves, wildflowers, shells, seeds, rocks, nuts, etc.

What You Do: Allow the children to classify their collections by color and by shape. Provide picture books, dictionaries, cut out pictures, seed catalogs, shell books and other resources for children to identify their collections.

What to Talk About: This depends on the collection.

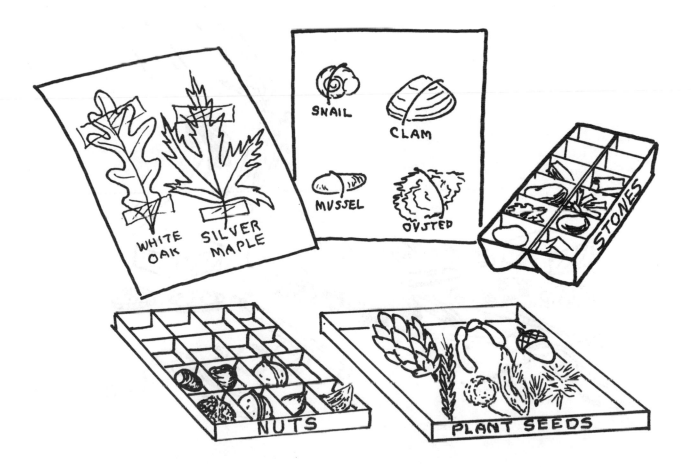

Magnets

What You Are Going to Teach: Properties of magnetism. Magnets will pick up only certain materials.

Materials Needed for Teaching: A large magnet. Several different objects made of different materials. Two plastic produce or meat trays.

What You Do: Encourage the children to spread the different objects out on a table. Let them explore with the magnet to see which objects it will pick up and which it won't pick up. What will it pick up? Will it pick up everything? Why not? Does it have anything to do with what the object is made of? Encourage the children to sort objects into labeled trays according to whether they attract the magnet or not.

What to Talk About: Discuss the materials that the magnet will pick up and materials that it will not pick up. Predict which materials in the classroom may be attracted. Test to see if the guesses are correct.

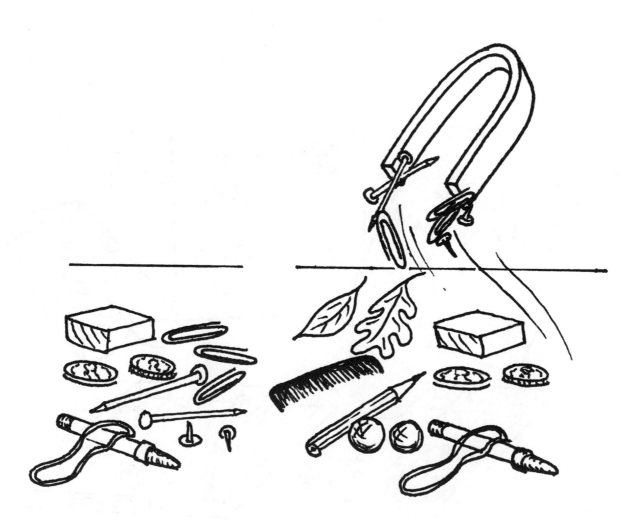

Growing Crystals

What You Are Going to Teach: Observation of the formation of crystals. Growing crystals.

Materials Needed for Teaching: Charcoal briskets, salt, ammonia, bluing, food coloring.

What You Do: Use an old pie pan or shallow glass dish. Break up charcoal and put in pan. Add to the charcoal two tablespoons each of water, salt, bluing and ammonia. As the liquid evaporates, the crystals will begin to grow. You may add color to this garden of crystals by adding a few drops of food color to the dish. You control the size of the crystals by the amount of the liquid solution you add.

What to Talk About: Crystal, bluing, salt, ammonia, solution, garden, charcoal. Provide additional information from the library on crystals.

Explanation of Principles: Crystals are formed as the solution of salt, bluing, ammonia, water, and charcoal evaporates (passes from a liquid to a gas). Different solutions form different shaped crystals. Often crystals of different types are used by industry. The structures of the crystals are determined by their chemical content. Children may observe the shape of the crystals with a magnifying glass.

Food Book

What You Are Going to Teach: Different foods taste different. Cooking makes a difference. Usually our taste determines whether we like a food or not.

Materials Needed for Teaching: Magazines, scissors, glue, magic marker, materials for making books (see Seed Book).

What You Do: Allow the children to go through the magazines and select pictures of foods or dishes they like or dislike. Encourage the children to cut these out and glue into the book. Help the children (write what they say) record their feelings about the foods they have selected.

What to Talk About: Vocabulary words appropriate to foods selected.

Using a Balance Scale

What You Are Going to Teach: Objects have different weights. Meaning of "heavier than." Meaning of "lighter than." Objects may be classified according to weight.

Materials Needed for Teaching: A simple balance scale, an assortment of objects to be weighed.

What You Do: Introduce the children (individually or in small groups) to the balance scale. After the children have become familiar with the scale, allow them to compare weights and sizes of various objects. Let the children select one object and sort the remaining things according to which are heavier, lighter, or weigh the same as their initial selection.

What to Talk About: Scale, lighter, heavier, chart, balance, weigh, weight, same, sort.

Teacher Reference Books

Bennett, Lloyd. **STIFES, Science Teachers Information for Elementary School.** Texas: Texas Woman's University, 1976.

Bonsall, George. **How and Why Wonder Book of Weather.** New York: Wonder Books, 1960.

Brown, Vinson. **How to Make a Miniature Zoo.** Boston: Little, Brown, 1957.

Cobb, Vicki. **More Science Experiments You Can Eat.** New York: Lippincott, 1979.

Cooper, Elizabeth K. **Science in Your Own Backyard.** New York: Harcourt, Brace, 1960.

Craig, Jean. **Questions and Answers About Weather.** New York: Scholastic Book Services, 1969.

Croft, Doreen. **An Activities Handbook for Teachers of Young Children.** Boston: Houghton Mifflin Co., 1975.

Davis, Arnold and Miller, Donald. **Science Games.** California: Fearon, 1974.

de Regniers, Beatrice Schenck; Moore, Eva; and White, Mary. **Poems Children Will Sit Still For.** New York: Scholastic Book Services, 1973.

Eliason, Claudia Fuhriman, and Jenkins, Lou Thomson. **A Practical Guide to Early Childhood Curriculum.** St. Louis: C.V. Mosby Co., 1977.

Fleming, Bonnie Mack and Hamilton, Darlene Softley. **Resources for Creative Teaching in Early Childhood Education.** New York: Harcourt, Brace, Jovanich, Inc., 1969.

Forte, Imogene and MacKenzie, Joy. **Creative Science Experiences for the Young Child.** Tennessee: Incentive Publications, 1973.

Freeman, Mae. **The Real Book of Magnets.** New York: Scholastic Book Services, 1967.

Green, Ivah. **Animals Under Your Feet.** Penn.: Laurel Press, 1958.

Harlan, Jean Durgin. **Science Experiments for the Early Childhood Years.** Ohio: Merrill, 1976.

Holden, Raymond. **Magnetism.** New York: Golden Press, 1962.

Holl, Adelaide. **Listening for Sounds.** Indianapolis: Bobbs-Merrill, Inc., 1970.

Keen, Martin. **How and Why Wonder Book of Science Experiments.** New York: Wonder Books, 1962.

Kushin, Rochelle. **The Kindergarten Box—A Treasury of Ideas for the Teacher.** Calif.: Educational Insights, 1978.

Lang, Donald. **Let's Go Sciencing, Resource Series No. 37.** Indiana: MPAT, Inc., 1969.

Munson, Howard R. **Science Activities with Simple Things.** Calif.: Fearon-Pitman, 1962.

Parker, Bertha Morris. **Nature Wonderland.** Indianapolis: Bobbs-Merrill Co., 1970.

Parker, Bertha. **The Wonders of Science.** Indianapolis: Bobbs-Merrill Co., 1970.

Pine, Tillie, and Levine, Joseph. **Water All Around.** New York: Whittlesey House, 1959.

Pondendorf, Illa. **True Book of Magnets and Electricity.** Chicago: Children's Press, 1972.

Reuben, Gabriel, and Archer, Gloria. **What is A Magnet?** Chicago: Benefit Press, 1959.

Roy, Mary Massey. **Probe, A Handbook for Teachers of Elementary Science.** Michigan: Educational Service, Inc., 1962.

Russell, Helen Ross. **Ten-Minute Field Trips: Using the School Grounds for Environmental Studies.** Chicago: J.G. Ferguson, 1973.

Science Teaching Guide—Level K. Curriculum Guide for Plano Independent School District, 1979.

Sharp, Elizabeth. **Simple Machines and How They Work.** New York: Random House, 1959.

Shuttlesworth, Dorothy. **The Story of Rocks.** New York: Doubleday and Co., 1966.

Van Amerongen, C. **The Way Things Work: An Illustrated Encyclopedia of Technology.** New York: Simon & Schuster, 1969.

White, Anne Terry. **Rocks All Around Us.** New York: Scholastic Book Services, 1959.

Wyler, Rose, and Ames, Gerald. **Prove It.** New York: Scholastic Book Services, 1967.